TABLE OF CONTENTS

FIRST THINGS FIRST	02
STRATEGY	
Marketing & Communication Strategies	03
Market Research & Competitive Intelligence	07
Campaign Planning & Execution	15
Reporting	19
MARKETING & SALES	
Lead Generation	20
Sales Enablement & Marketing Automation	21
Coordination with Sales	24
TEAM	
Managing Marketing Teams	25
Managing Sales Teams	26
Training	27
ADVERTISING	
Paid Media, PPC & Social	28
Email Marketing	30
Product Presentations	31
CONTENT	
Content Marketing	34
Web, Search Engine Optimisation & Analytics	36
Marketing Collateral	37
Organic Social	39
DEVELOPMENT	
Project Management	40
New Products & Services	41
Evaluation & Adjustment	42
Managing External Agencies & Partners	43
WRAPPING IT UP	44

rusty@gimaev.com.au

RUSTY GIMAEV
YOUR MARKETING GURU

www.gimaev.com.au

FIRST THINGS FIRST

I'm not here to waste your time. If you're looking for a quick and easy way to absorb the practical knowledge you need to successfully build and market your business, this is the guide for you. I have condensed my 20+ years of experience managing talented marketing teams, hundreds of successfully implemented projects, and millions of dollars spent on marketing into a complete handbook that you can read in less than half an hour.

Rather than lengthy descriptions and dense theory, these pages offer clear, ready to implement, time proven hacks that will help grow your business and boost your revenue from day one.

The key areas covered in this guide include building an effective marketing strategy, marketing and sales, team management, advertising, content marketing, development and project management.

> No more words – let's get straight to growing your business!

STRATEGY
MARKETING & COMMUNICATION STRATEGIES

What even is marketing?

Marketing is both an art and a science. It is your proactive and strategic mission of reaching potential buyers for your product or service, with the intention of making a profit.

All business success relies on solving a problem for people or meeting a need. So the aim of marketing is to identify the people who want or need what you're offering, and to convince them that your product or service will solve their problem or make their life better in some way.

rusty@gimaev.com.au

RUSTY GIMAEV
YOUR MARKETING GURU

www.gimaev.com.au

The marketing journey is an experience.

More than just making a sale, your mission with a marketing strategy is to take people by the hand and walk them through the full journey from discovering the product exists, to wanting it, buying it, and enjoying the difference it makes to their lives.

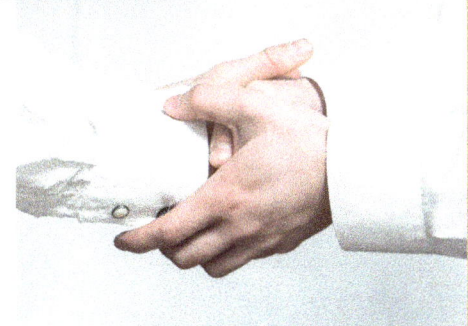

You need to think about the experience your customers are having from their very first contact with you, because this is all part of the journey. This means that your marketing strategy should focus on your customer's problems, pain points and frustrations, but also their hopes and desires.

Identify the best channels to reach your audience.

A marketing channel is just a route of connection or a means of communication with your customers. Different channels are more effective with different demographics – for example, mobile apps and social media platforms such as TikTok are a good way to reach younger customers, while older groups are more likely to prefer email.

Offer real value.

We talk about value for money, but the real value of your product or service is about more than the price they pay for it. Think of value as benefit to the customer, or improvement on the status quo. How much has your product helped them, benefited them, or solved their frustrations?

Something relatively inexpensive can be of great value to the customer if it meets a specific need or solves a problem. In the same way, something can be hugely expensive to buy and actually offer very little value or benefit to the customer (buyer's remorse, anyone?).

The real value that you provide includes the customer's experience throughout the whole buying process, and in all of their contact and interactions with you. This adds value to your offering (and justifies charging more for it).

The bulk of marketing is about helping your customers to understand the real value that you're offering. A top tip for getting people's attention and encouraging them to listen is to create an enticing sense that you have something they need, or that will greatly improve their life in some way, and you want to share it with them. They have to believe that what you hold in your hands is worth something to them, otherwise they won't lean in to find out more.

Identify your short, mid and long term marketing goals.

Knowing where you want to get to is half the job. As you would with the GPS navigation in your car, start with your destination in mind. Write down your short, mid and long term marketing goals so that you know what to strive towards, and what success will look like. This will also enable your internal navigation system and creative mind to think about the ways to get there.

Example:

SHORT TERM GOALS:
- Expand further into overseas and interstate markets wanting to invest in QLD properties
- 8 Offices throughout South East Queensland within 3 to 5 years

MID – LONG TERM GOALS:
- Open offices interstate within the next 5 years
- Open interior design and home staging department

It's also useful to write what you don't want to do.

Example:
- No plans for other more remote locations (Cairns, Mackay)

> Use this information to create your effective and comprehensive marketing strategy.

MARKETING RESEARCH & COMPETITIVE INTELLIGENCE

Learn from others.

Successful marketing is a lot more about effort, drive and strategy than it is about big budgets. If you're smart and strategic in your marketing, you can use whatever budget you have in the most effective and targeted way.

It always pays to learn by example – both good and bad! Look at the digital marketing strategies of your competitors, including leaders in your industry who are clearly doing something right. Pay special attention to those brands that have cultivated an active and loyal online following as this is such a powerful asset in modern marketing.

Define key personas for your business and identify high priorities.

You can focus your energy and resources in the most effective way by directing your attention towards those people who are most ready and willing to buy your product. You can waste a lot of time and resources trying to reach disengaged people who are very unlikely to ever buy your product – either because they don't have the available resources, or it's just not a high enough priority or pain point for them.

This is why it's important to identify some key potential buyers for your product, who will be most motivated and easiest to convert into sales, and to focus your marketing energies on reaching these people. We call these 'key personas'.

Key personas are basically different types of customers.

Strategy - Market Research & Competitive Intelligence   08

The more you know about them, the better – this will guide you in finding the best approach for connecting with them, generating interest in your products and services, selling to them, and maintaining the relationship so that they can recommend your business to others.

The easiest way to get started is to categorise the main personas by the type of products or services they need.

Example: Key personas for a real estate agency.

5 KEY PERSONAS IDENTIFIED:
- Property sellers (1)
- Property buyers (2)
    - First homeowners (2A) • Investors (2B)
- Landlords (3) for property management
- Renters (4)
- New real estate agents (5)

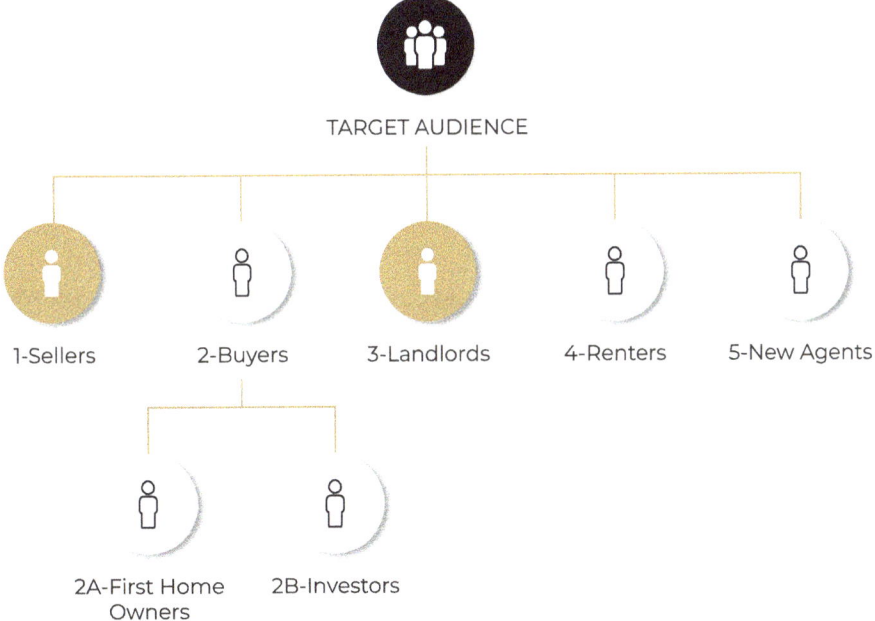

TARGET AUDIENCE

1-Sellers   2-Buyers   3-Landlords   4-Renters   5-New Agents

2A-First Home Owners   2B-Investors

rusty@gimaev.com.au   RUSTY GIMAEV   YOUR MARKETING GURU   www.gimaev.com.au

Strategy - Market Research & Competitive Intelligence

While all types of customers are important, your business might prioritise some over others. In the example above, the real estate agency's key personas (who generate most of the revenue) are likely to be **sellers of property** and **landlords** wishing to rent out their properties. While, for a buyer's agency, the key personas might be **buyers of the property** as they are the ones who pay the agency fee.

Knowing what type of customers you are most interested in in a business sense will help you to build your marketing strategy around them, so that you spend most of your resources (money, time, etc) on getting the right customers in the most efficient way (and avoid spending time on those things that are 'good to have' but not critical to your success).

You can even dig deeper and define the characteristics of each persona, noting details such as age, geolocation, job, education, etc. This could further help you to target your potential audience when advertising on paid media, writing new content, etc.

Example:
Personas for real estate agency.

	Sellers	Buyers	Landlords	Renters	New agents
Geolocation					
Age bracket					
Qualification					
Job role					
Notes					

Strategy - Market Research & Competitive Intelligence

Note key geographical areas for your business.

Understanding geotargeting is crucial for keyword analysis, SEO and paid media planning.

Identify which areas your existing or potential customers mostly come from. This could be a radius around your head office, e.g. 5-10 km in every direction.

It can be helpful to create a list of suburbs.

Example:
- Albany Creek
- Aspley
- Bald Hills
- Bracken Ridge
- Bridgeman Downs
- Carseldine
- Chermside
- Chermside West
- Fitzgibbon
- McDowell
- Taigum

If you are running or planning to run paid media campaigns, internally or via an external agency, this list will help you to include only those areas that are most likely to generate good leads for you. And if your budget is limited, it is strategically sensible to **exclude areas** other than your target area. This will help to maximise the potential of your budget and generate leads that are most likely to convert.

rusty@gimaev.com.au
RUSTY GIMAEV
YOUR MARKETING GURU
www.gimaev.com.au

Strategy - Market Research & Competitive Intelligence

Spend some time on competitor analysis.

Analysing what your competitors are doing will help you to build an effective marketing strategy and win a bigger market share, attracting new customers and swaying existing clients over to you.

Identify your strong and weak points, and those of your competitors – at least on a high level.

Example: Company ABC

POSITIVE
- Well structured
- Extensive training
- Reward system
- Good advertising

NEGATIVE
- Do or die attitude
- Leads are going to top tier
- Toxic culture

RUSTY GIMAEV
YOUR MARKETING GURU

Identify critical success factors.

You can take this a step further and create a table of critical success factors. These are the things that matter most to customers when they decide to buy your product or services. Each factor can be assigned a different weight of importance. For example, faster delivery might be more highly valued by customers than a slight difference in price.

1-5 (1 – minimum, 5 – maximum score)

Critical Success Factor	Weight	Company A	Company B	Company C
Recommendations & references				
Online reviews				
Location				
Experience / track record				
Industry memberships				
Good communication				
Credentials, training, certificates				
Pricing / fees				
Marketing costs & ROI				
Delivery				
Website quality				
Range of additional services				

This table can be a helpful way of highlighting strong points and areas for improvement. It also makes sense to create critical success factors for each core product or service (e.g. Property sales, Property management, etc.)

rusty@gimaev.com.au

RUSTY GIMAEV
YOUR MARKETING GURU

www.gimaev.com.au

Find out what is currently being offered to your target audience.

Example:
- Marketing kit
- Software & Training
- External trainers
- Good relationships
- Base + Commission for first 12 months

Find out key reasons or motivators to switch.

Think about why your competitors' customers might switch to you.

Example:
- Inspiring change
- Conflict
- Better opportunities
- Better pay structure
- Innovative marketing
- Better training
- More help and support

Identify barriers to switching.

Example:
- Not aware of the differences between brands

Analyse what can be done to improve your offering.

Think about ways to improve your offering, making sure customers understand the benefits you provide and your point of difference. Talk about the actual benefits and problems you solve, rather than the specs of your product or services.

Stand out from the crowd.

It is very unlikely that you are the only company doing what you do. There are probably multiple similar products to yours on the market, so your potential customers have a choice –
and you want them to choose you.

This means you need to create and highlight your points of difference – show them why your company, your product or your offering is different to the many others out there, and why they should choose you. You need to give your customers some solid reasons to buy from you rather than your competitors. One approach is to set your company apart as a leading expert, using your industry experience and expertise to create valuable resources for your customers – detailed online guides, for example.

Potential customers can only form an opinion about your company and your product based on the image you present to them through your website, marketing, customer service and sales experience. This is how they will compare you to your competitors. This is one of the reasons why a strong and coherent marketing strategy is so important, and can't just be an afterthought. You might have the greatest product in the world, but if your website, communications and marketing materials are second rate, potential customers won't even get that far. The good news is that all of this is in your hands!

Again – marketing is a journey and an experience, and it is all part of the value that you offer to potential customers. It can help to find out what your existing or past customers have appreciated most about their experience of your company, and start to turn them into brand ambassadors.

Know where not to spend your efforts.

Some products and services can be government subsidised so that the end user can get them for free, or with a significant discount. Do your research and see if you can get approved for government subsidies. If not, reallocate your advertising budget and efforts to marketing other products.

CAMPAIGN PLANNING & EXECUTION

Think about your goals and calls to action.

The primary goals of advertising campaigns are usually lead generation and sales. Raising brand awareness can also be a factor, but businesses usually want to turn invested advertising budget into actual revenue.

At the planning stage it is important to decide on what call to action to use. In some cases, testing is essential to see if the campaign will actually work. Thankfully, testing can be done within a short time and with a relatively small budget. If a campaign fails to generate several leads within the test period, it is time to go back to the drawing board and change the call to action or the campaign's angle.

A common mistake is to assume that people will be interested to 'learn about your business'. By default, people are generally not interested in your business unless you show them why they should be – whether it is a problem you can help them to solve or a product or service that could improve their lives.

The call to action shouldn't be vague. For example, in a real estate context, a free consultation by a real estate agent turned out to be a weak value proposition compared to a property appraisal campaign. Visitors appeared to be more interested in discovering how much their property was worth than getting free advice. This was valuable learning.

Some ideas for calls to action:

- Enquire now
- Coupons
- Download information pack
- Giveaways (free books, etc)
- Special offers (free property styling when you list property for sale with us)

Tips for an effective online campaign.

Once the idea for the campaign is clear – for example, a 'What's my property worth?' campaign for a real estate agency – it's important to follow some steps:

EXTENSIVE KEYWORD RESEARCH to find possible combinations of words (keywords) people might use to find your offer.

BUILD MASTER LANDING PAGE for the top keyword.
It's important to include the top keyword in the title of the pages and multiple times throughout the body, where relevant.

Ideally, a form to collect users' data needs to be above the fold so that it's visible. This form shouldn't ask for too much information – just the basics, such as name, email, phone. Statistically, the more fields you add, the fewer people will complete it. Obviously, if some information is critical to your offer (e.g. property address for a property appraisal) you should include this field. But try to balance your desire to know more about the lead with what is absolutely required. You can always fill in the gaps when you communicate with the customer later.

USE A CLEAR CALL TO ACTION
Your call to action should be clear and large so that people can make sense of the page within one or two seconds. If the offer is unclear or vague, people will just leave the page without providing their contact details and this is a potential lead lost.

DON'T UNDERESTIMATE THE VALUE OF SOCIAL PROOF

Personal recommendations, testimonials, and recognised awards can go a long way in making potential customers feel warmly towards you. Nobody wants to feel like you're testing your product out on them – social proof builds trust and confidence.

You can include case studies, certifications, and even detailed letters of recommendation from satisfied customers to prove that what you say about your company and your offering is true.

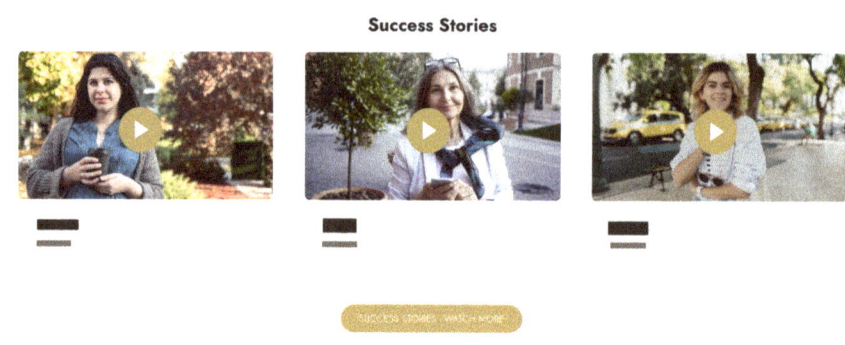

TEST SHORT VS LONG LANDING PAGE

Some people will tell you that it's never a good idea to have a very long landing page, with a lot of information to absorb. But, in some cases, long pages do work and convert if the information provided actually helps to convince users (testimonials, videos, etc). Consider doing A/B testing to see if a shorter or longer version works better.

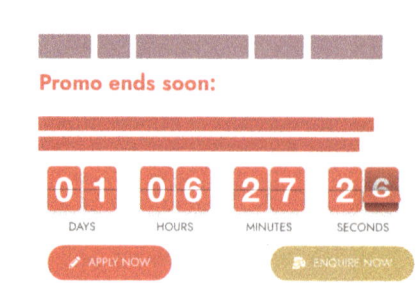

CREATE A SENSE OF URGENCY

A visual sense of urgency can help to turn a good landing page into a brilliant converting tool. This could mean including a countdown timer that changes on the page in real time. It could count down to the end of a promotion, or could show

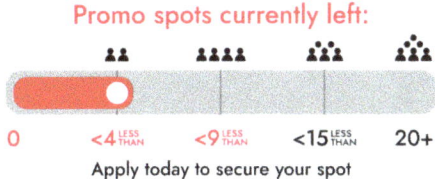

number of promotional spots remaining, or both. People don't like the feeling of missing out on something and usually act faster if there is a driver for them to take action now. It's important not to set the countdown timer to a date that's too far into the future – 'Promo ends in 60 days' is not as effective as 'Promo ends in 5 days'. If you are selling something that requires longer to reach a buying decision (e.g. complex equipment, where many stakeholders are involved), you can tweak your call to action so that people just need to enquire by a certain date to benefit from the offer. You can still add T&Cs around a purchase date if required, but at least this way you will gain a potential customer's contact details instead of missing out.

SHOW THE DIFFERENCE BETWEEN PROMO AND 'NORMAL' PRICE

If you are running a promotion, where the price of the product or service is discounted, don't just list the new price. If you include both prices, this clearly communicates to customers that they will get a good deal if they act fast.

USE ONE OR TWO CALLS TO ACTION ONLY

It is not a good idea to use more than two calls to action. For example, you can have an 'Enquire now' form at the top of the page and 'Download information pack' at the bottom. Make sure you make it possible for people to download something for free – this is a nice, low risk call to action for visitors and you can still get their names and emails.

OPTIMISE LANDING PAGES FOR KEYWORDS

Once you have a master template for the landing page, you can consider creating variations of the same page, tailored specifically to your main groups of keywords. This could make your campaign more effective by increasing the quality score and exposure, reducing cost per click and cost per lead.

CREATE COMPELLING AD COPY

When advertising on Google Ads or other platforms, use ad copy that contains keyword(s) and a clear call to action, highlighting a brief statement about why users should take an action and what benefit it will provide for them.

Running offline campaigns.

Not all campaigns are online. Some industries require businesses to contact potential customers through a range of offline channels.

For example, in the real estate industry, you might have printed flyers delivered to specific areas every month to remind customers about your brand. You can create a calendar of letterbox drops for the year and work towards getting your marketing materials created and delivered.

REPORTING

Build automated reports that show some KPIs such as marketing spend, number of leads, cost per lead, cost per customer, revenue and ROI. This could save hours of manual work and will give you a bigger picture so that you can make data driven decisions.

MARKETING & SALES
LEAD GENERATION

Lead generation is one of the most important goals of marketing. By generating more high quality leads you can build the pipeline of future customers and drive your business growth.

If you need leads to start coming straight away, get a Google Ads or other paid media campaign running. Start with **search campaigns** as they are targeting people who are actively searching for a product or service like yours.

Consider whether your current website needs a refresh or major redevelopment to stay in line with the competition and attract new customers. Does it provide a great user experience? Is it mobile friendly? Can people easily find what they're looking for? Does your website represent your brand in the best light?

Think about ways to get more word-of-mouth referrals and attract **brand ambassadors**.

Launch an **affiliate program** to drive more traffic and generate more leads for your business.

SALES ENABLEMENT & MARKETING AUTOMATION

The primary goal of marketing is to make sure that you are the obvious choice for anyone who might be looking for the products and services you offer, so that potential customers choose you over the competition and ultimately spend their money on your offering. How successful you are in achieving this will come down to the strength of your marketing efforts.

Approach sales as a process.

It's important to think about sales as a process, not just a point of exchange. It's much easier to encourage potential customers to take multiple small steps that feel minor and non-committal (micro-commitments) than to go in for the hard sell from the get-go. In this way, you are gradually leading them towards an action or purchase and not scaring them off before they feel ready to make the commitment.

This means engaging with potential customers as they research, consider, compare products, and ask questions. Demonstrate that you are available and ready to help, and won't pressure them to take the plunge until they feel comfortable and ready. This means friendly, regular contact, and always following up to find out what you can do next to help the customer make their decision. You are helping, supporting and leading them by the hand towards an action, while allowing it to be their own, informed decision.

At the same time, you can encourage potential customers in the right direction by offering some sort of incentive (a limited time promo, a free ebook or a giveaway). If you give people something that is genuinely useful or practical, you are likely to position yourself in their minds as a helpful supporter and an insightful guide, even if they don't immediately make a purchase. This makes them more likely to come back to you when they're ready.

Clearly and boldly invite customers to buy or take action.

Calls to action are a non-negotiable. If you don't make it clear to potential customers what you are asking them to do, they won't take the next step. Whether you want them to make a purchase, find out more, get in contact, or download a guide – make it clear and easy.

Consider automating certain processes.

Marketing automation systems such as HubSpot can dramatically change the way your business operates and increase efficiency. Automation can also ensure that you don't neglect potentially valuable leads.

The obvious place to start is with repeated actions that are currently being performed manually but could be done by an automated system, such as sending emails, SMS, creating tasks, etc.

For more complex processes, you can start by listing all the steps and putting them on a diagram to visualise the sequence. This makes it easier to identify possible dependencies.

Stay on top of your leads.

If you want all leads to be taken care of promptly and diligently, ensure that each one is assigned to a specific person rather than a team of people.

Don't let newly generated leads sit in your pipeline for long. If a salesperson is not able to call the lead straight away, you should at least ensure that there is an autoreply set up to acknowledge receipt of the message and provide the contact details of your sales team.

A well structured lead nurturing system is highly recommended for all businesses to keep in touch with your prospective customers and maximise your conversion rate.

Negotiate a good deal on your systems.

When signing up for a CRM / marketing automation software, don't forget to negotiate heavily and ask for a substantial discount – even as high as 60%. These platforms are highly motivated to gain new customers in this very competitive market and are therefore often ready to provide better than standard conditions for you to get started with them.

Plan systems carefully.

Deploying a new marketing automation or CRM system requires careful planning. It is especially important to identify what fields/properties you need to use to ensure that data integrity is fully maintained. This will allow you to filter your target audience, send personalised messages, etc.

COORDINATION WITH SALES

Support your sales team.

Ensure that your sales staff is 100% familiar with the products and services you are offering, as well as their benefits and features.

You can help your team by creating a professional sales pack that they use when doing presentations or selling. Having a brochure and some form of presentation template (which staff can customise to their needs) is a must. Provide them with as many marketing assets as possible – this could include brochures, flyers, 3D tours, product or service explanation videos, customer testimonials (both written and video), presentations, free giveaways, company merchandise, and more.

Think about ways to motivate salespeople by introducing a bonus plan that is both realistic and rewarding.

TEAM
MANAGING MARKETING TEAMS

Actively involve all team members and provide training to marketers, increasing the capabilities of the team to implement more complex tasks and with less supervision. This also makes it possible to delegate more tasks to junior team members.

Encourage team members to propose new ideas as these can often result in a number of improvements for customer satisfaction and overall efficiencies. Examples include a system for monitoring customer feedback, higher quality marketing materials, and improved communication.

rusty@gimaev.com.au   RUSTY GIMAEV — YOUR MARKETING GURU   www.gimaev.com.au

Give the bigger picture when assigning a specific task to a team member. Let them know where this task sits in the overall scheme of things and how it contributes to the success of the project. This simple step can not only make a huge difference to the person implementing the task, boosting motivation and removing unknowns, but will also ensure that the outcome of the task is aligned with the goal of the project.

Celebrate the small successes of your team, praise good work and show how important everyone's contribution is to the overall achievements and successes of the company.

MANAGING SALES TEAMS

Introduce a bonus scheme.

To maximise sales, increase lead-to-customer conversion, boost revenue, and shorten the sales cycle, it's a good idea to introduce an effective bonus scheme.

It's essential to set achievable goals that will motivate staff to achieve more. Don't set unattainable targets that will only discourage people. Avoid the trap of ever-increasing targets when a salesperson achieves them – shifting the goalposts like this will demotivate even highly determined sales staff.

Ideally, calculate a percentage of the total cost of the product or service and set it as a bonus.

Empower your team to sell.

Don't just expect magic from your sales team – provide them with an opportunity to sell more. Authorise your sales staff to provide on-the-spot discounts to leads that haven't converted within a set period of time, especially if you are selling digital products or services that do not bear material costs. These are leads you have already spent time and money on so it's worth doing what you can to get something in return for this investment.

If you are nervous about your sales team offering all products or services at a high discount to secure maximum sales, set rules for when this can happen (for example, after one month) and link their bonus to the amount sold.

TRAINING

Properly training your staff allows you to delegate more tasks and take care of the 'bigger picture'. It also means your teams are more confident, motivated and effective in their work.

Create training materials.

Save hours of your time and facilitate a quicker and smoother start for new employees by creating how-to guides, manuals and training programs. Document important processes and include key screenshots and even brief videos.

Save all files and share them when doing an induction for new staff.

Seek out educational content and opportunities for your staff going forwards, so that they can upskill themselves. This will benefit individual employees, departmental teams, your customers, and the company as a whole.

ADVERTISING

Identify the most fruitful sources and channels.

It's a good idea to try and keep a log of where your customers have come from. How did they find you? Which channel brought them to you or your website? This helps you to identify the most effective (and therefore profitable) marketing channels so that you can focus your resources in the right place – for maximum returns.

PAID MEDIA, PPC & SOCIAL

Monitor cost per lead.

While there are many metrics to measure a campaign's performance, one of the most important ones is cost per lead. It is calculated by dividing money spent by number of leads.

Depending on the industry, product, call to action, and quality of the campaign, cost per lead can vary from as low as $10 to $100+.

rusty@gimaev.com.au RUSTY GIMAEV www.gimaev.com.au
YOUR MARKETING GURU

If cost per lead is currently high, there are a number of things you can do to bring it down:

- Improve quality of the landing page
- Use highly targeted ad groups
- Pause/disable expensive ad groups
- Consider changing call to action
- Add a limited time promotion with a timer
- Ensure 3 components (keywords, ad copies and landing pages) are well aligned

Start small.

When launching a new campaign, start with a smaller budget – say, 25% of the normal daily budget – and then increase it if the campaign performs well.

When advertising through social media channels, try using a freebie to generate leads.

EMAIL MARKETING

Email marketing is one of the easiest and most effective tools to reach wider audiences. You can reach thousands of people at once, track performance (open and click rate) and make a real difference to your sales and revenue.

Be consistent.

Many small businesses send one-off emails to customers, but it makes a huge difference if you set up some lead nurturing campaigns. These are basically a series of emails that every lead receives at a certain time interval. Lead generating emails should not be direct advertising but rather stories of how your products and services help people – so that your recipients can identify with these needs or pain points, and understand your value offering. By educating your audience about how their problems could be solved or life improved, you can promote your business and generate more sales in an effective way.

It makes sense to use one of the many email marketing tools or CRMs available on the market. Ideally, all forms on your website or landing pages should be pushing new leads to your CRM, where automation takes over to ensure that your leads are receiving important and valuable communications on 'autopilot'.

Find more business in follow ups.

It's a costly exercise to approach your leads just once, when they are generated, and not to remarket to them later. There is plenty of potential business to be generated from these older leads.

Utilise tools.

There are many different tools and solutions on the market for these purposes – some expensive, and others not so much. Some are even tailored for a specific industry (e.g. real estate), offering additional features such as including property listings into emails, etc.

Test and refine.

Do some A/B testing of the content and subject line if you're not sure what will resonate best with your audience, and then analyse the effectiveness of each different approach. To improve the open rate, always personalise your emails by including the first name of the recipient in the subject line as well as the email body.

PRODUCT PRESENTATIONS

Create effective presentations.

Facilitate the production of accessible, informative and engaging visual presentation materials. If you don't produce great presentation materials, your products and services could end up being presented in a way that doesn't do them justice.

Make sure your sales and marketing teams have the most up-to-date materials that are tailored for your target audience – not too complex or technical to turn people off, but enough to show how your product and services could help them solve their issues or improve their lives.

Take people out of their environment.

It is a proven observation that people are more likely to act, buy, or spend more when they feel relaxed and are out of their normal routine – for example, when travelling or attending a one-off, in-person event. People seem to feel more optimistic, emboldened and generous in this context. Simply providing refreshments at an event could boost conversions by about 20%!

If you want to maximise revenue, there is a strong argument for taking people out of their everyday environment and giving them a good time at an offline event.

Encourage active participation.

People are much more likely to stay switched on and engaged, and to remember the takeaways, if you get them involved in a presentation in some way. Don't just share knowledge and information, but give your audience an experience. This might include questions, dialogue, role play, humour – whatever it is, involve your audience and get creative. Storytelling is a powerful tool for making the experience memorable and moving your audience to action – people don't like a pushy salesperson, but we all love a good story.

Radiate confidence.

Your own attitude will be instrumental in dictating the outcome of your presentation. Anticipate success and go after it. Have confidence in yourself and your abilities to communicate and persuade, but also have complete confidence in the product. Your enthusiasm and excitement will be contagious.

Be an example.

When possible and appropriate, show your audience that you personally believe in the value of the product and that you can vouch for how much it has benefited you. Put yourself on a level with your audience, showing that you empathise with their needs, desires or frustrations, and that you have found a winning solution that you want to share with them. For example, if you were marketing an Apple Watch, you would wear one during the presentation.

CONTENT
CONTENT MARKETING

Create an effective content marketing strategy.

This should include a high volume of unique and engaging digital content for the website and social media, landing pages, infographics, presentations, flyers, promo videos and educational videos.

Remember that your communication needs to be aligned with your branding.

Think about what key messages you would like your audience to take away from your communication and build your comms strategy around these.

Online users want instant, relevant and high quality information, based on their search term. This can include:

- Essential product information
- Product features and benefits, clearly outlined
- Images of product, and brief explanations of USPs
- Technical specifications and demo videos
- Product comparisons
- Case studies and testimonials from other customers
- Independent product reviews
- Quick start guides and tutorials
- White papers
- Expert interviews
- FAQs
- Email newsletters
- Press releases

---

rusty@gimaev.com.au

RUSTY GIMAEV
YOUR MARKETING GURU

www.gimaev.com.au

Harness happy customers.

When you get positive feedback and compliments from satisfied customers, ask for their permission to share their comments. These could be instrumental in converting more sales, therefore turning an intangible asset into actual revenue.

Don't name competitors.

Focus on your brand and product, your USPs and points of difference, and the value you offer, and don't name specific competitors. Keep the attention on the positives – the relative benefits and advantages of your products and services – and let that speak for itself.

Keep it simple.

Don't try to be too clever or sound too sophisticated. Keep it simple and straightforward so that your potential customers can quickly understand exactly what you have to offer. Make it as easy as possible for people to grasp the key messages, and keep it friendly and accessible. Your audience will thank you!

WEB, SEARCH ENGINE OPTIMISATION & ANALYTICS

You only have 3 seconds.

Subconsciously, we give a website only 3 seconds to grab our attention before we decide to move on. Your landing page needs to engage a potential buyer in that first 3 second window, and then work to hold their attention beyond that. The journey from visitor to active customer might not happen overnight, but it all starts in those first crucial seconds.

Make sure that your website looks professional and appealing. A modern website must offer a great user experience – fast and mobile friendly, with plenty of visual content.

Refine user experience.

Use tools like Hotjar to analyse user behaviour when visiting your website. Think about how you can improve the user experience, making it easier for your audience to see what you are doing and how to benefit from your offering.

Optimise landing pages.

When building landing pages, make sure that you optimise them both for conversions (human friendly) and for search engines. If using Google Ads, strive for a 10 out of 10 quality score for your primary keywords. This can dramatically reduce cost per click and cost per lead, and increase conversion rate and overall ROI for campaigns.

Turn your website into a sales machine.

Your website should be constantly functioning as a sales machine, generating views, clicks, enquiries, and leads that can be converted into customers. This usually involves multiple stages of communication and interaction, carefully crafted to achieve that tangible and measurable output.

Tell your audience what to do.

It sounds obvious, but don't assume that your audience knows what you want them to do. Make it clear, and show them how easy it is to take the next step.

MARKETING COLLATERAL

Branding

Whether you are rebranding your existing business or creating new branding, it is important to get some fundamental things decided, designed and produced.

These might include:

- Brand colours
- Fonts/Typography
- Logo
- Tagline or slogan
- Business cards
- Letterhead
- Email signature
- Office signage
- Social media templates

Brand values and positioning.

Aside from tangible brand assets, you might think about some intangible things such as identifying your brand values and brand positioning. In other words, how do you want your business to be perceived by your customers, and what are your points of difference in comparison with the competition? This will help you to build your communication strategy with your customers, identify priorities in the customer service area, and guide other important decisions.

Examples of marketing assets include:

- Company brochure
- Flyers
- Ebooks
- Educational videos
- Bus stop advertising
- Landing pages
- Presentations

ORGANIC SOCIAL

Carefully plan and implement a social media calendar.
Consider launching a number of contests. This will help to cultivate a high level of engagement and generate new leads. Social media channels are powerful tools in raising brand awareness for your business. Potential customers will often check your social media channels as a very first port of call these days, to see if the business is operational and credible. If the last post is dated a year ago, that's going to be a serious deterrent for a customer to contact you or order your product or service.

If you don't have a dedicated person in your team to look after social media posting, delegate a task of publishing at least one post every fortnight.

Here are some topics for social media posts:

- **Products or services:** Photos and videos highlighting your products and services.
- **Customer testimonials:** Showcasing reviews and positive experiences from our clients.
- **Contests & campaigns:** For example, a 'Guess the Sale Price' campaign, etc.
- **Holidays/long weekends:** New Year, Christmas, Mother's Day, etc.
- **Tips:** Offering valuable insights to your audience.
  Market update posts
- **Company Updates:** Sharing news and updates about our team, awards, or notable milestones
- Staff Work Anniversaries
- Staff Birthdays
- Office Anniversary
- Company magazine
- **Events post:** award night, festivals, etc.
- Blog posts
- Educational articles, how-to guides

As with all aspects of marketing, it is a good idea to check out what other companies in your industry are doing. You can follow some of your most successful competitors with your personal Facebook, Instagram or LinkedIn account and monitor their activities online.

DEVELOPMENT
PROJECT MANAGEMENT

Organise tasks.

Introduce a project management tool such as ClickUp to facilitate more effective and fruitful collaboration between teams. This will undoubtedly result in a faster implementation rate for projects.

Collect feedback.

Implement a system to collect feedback and ratings via staff signatures, using tools such as Customer Thermometer, and utilise automation to encourage more Google reviews. This can result in achieving a high NPS score and more reviews generated.

Implement an affiliate and loyalty program.

This can lead to a significant increase in business volume via word-of-mouth recommendations.

Revise all software.

Consider all of the tools and software that your company uses and see if you can replace 2-3 different similar solutions with one more powerful software option. Renegotiate deals with existing subscriptions by asking for additional discounts.

NEW PRODUCTS & SERVICES

Prioritise products to push to market and supervise marketing approaches for all major product launches. If possible, try running advertising campaigns for products in question to assess demand before getting these products into production or spending lots of money in development.

See if you can integrate certain processes and reduce the amount of work that has to be done manually. Often, simple processes are being done in the same way for years, while integration could easily save hundreds of hours.

EVALUATION & ADJUSTMENT

Nurture a positive reputation.

In today's digital, interconnected world, it matters more than ever that people are saying good things about you. Word spreads, and public opinion holds great weight. Pay attention to your reputation – online and offline – and do everything you can to improve your public image. One of the keys to this is giving a prompt and proactive response to any unsatisfied customers, as well as sharing as many positive reviews and testimonials as possible.

Analyse the customer journey.

Put yourself in your customers' shoes and find out for yourself what their experience is like. Is the customer journey smooth and enjoyable? Eliminate all possible roadblocks that could get in the way of customers ordering your products or services.

Utilise data from Google analytics, Google Ads, HubSpot or other systems to come up with a plan for further improving on key metrics.

Implement systems to track user behaviour.

Tracking is important so that you can understand how users are engaging with you, and better provide customers with relevant information via social media, AI chatbots, lead nurturing, direct emails, SMS messaging, letterbox dropping, and a quarterly magazine.

Implement a strategy for continuous improvement.

This is important for helping you to achieve an excellent Net Promoter Score, positive reviews, and more word-of-mouth recommendations.

Test, test, test!

Marketing doesn't have to be a guessing game. Some initiatives are more effective than others, but you can solve this mystery by testing your approaches. Testing will give you quantifiable evidence for which marketing initiatives are generating the best returns. The good news is that even a failed marketing attempt will add to your learning and help you to improve.

This will be a constant journey of trial and error, learning and adapting. Keep trying new things and testing new ideas, learning from successful brands, and refreshing your approaches.

MANAGING EXTERNAL AGENCIES & PARTNERS

Delegate projects that your internal team does not have the capacity or time to get done. Things like graphic design, web development, repeated admin tasks, and many other jobs could easily be delegated to external agencies or freelancers.

See if you can find a talented graphic designer, a web developer or another expert in a country that has a lower pay rate. Provided you brief people properly and manage the project well, you can get valuable work done and pay a fraction of the cost that you would normally pay locally.

WRAPPING IT UP

I hope that you have found this book useful, practical and inspiring, and that you feel fired up to start applying some of these proven marketing principles to your business today. These insights and techniques have already helped numerous businesses that I have worked with across Australia, and worldwide, and I am confident that you too will reap the benefits of my decades of experience and marketing dollars spent. That is my hope in sharing this with you, and I would love to hear how you get on.

For the very latest marketing tips, useful checklists and free downloadables, you can visit my personal website at **www.gimaev.com.au** or follow me on social media.

Need further advice or help with your projects?
Contact me today on **rusty@gimaev.com.au**

Let's keep in touch via LinkedIn **www.linkedin.com/in/rusgim/**

Thanks for reading, and I wish you every success!

Photos: Envato Elements (elements.envato.com), Freepik (freepik.com)

Disclaimer

This guide is intended to for general informational purposes and does not take into account your personal circumstances, needs or objectives. You are advised to seek professional advice from a qualified adviser before making any significant decisions. Although this publication has been compiled with care and attention to accuracy, neither the authors, publishers nor their employees can be held liable for errors or omissions. The publishers take no responsibility for any factors arising after the release of this guide that subsequently affect the relevance or accuracy of the information provided. The content within this guide is subject to change at any time. The reproduction or reprinting of any part of this guide, without the written permission of the author and the publisher, is an infringement of Copyright. The content does not necessarily reflect the opinions of the publisher.